ROCK

AND

TREE

SHARON SMULDERS WILLIAMS

Balboa Press books may be ordered through booksellers or by contacting:

Balboa Press
A Division of Hay House
1663 Liberty Drive
Bloomington, IN 47403
www.balboapress.com
1 (877) 407-4847

Because of the dynamic nature of the Internet, any web addresses or links contained in this book may have changed since publication and may no longer be valid. The views expressed in this work are solely those of the author and do not necessarily reflect the views of the publisher, and the publisher hereby disclaims any responsibility for them.

Any people depicted in stock imagery provided by Thinkstock are models, and such images are being used for illustrative purposes only. Certain stock imagery © Thinkstock.

ISBN: 978-1-5043-0856-4 (sc)
ISBN: 978-1-5043-0857-1 (e)

Print information available on the last page.

Balboa Press rev. date: 11/23/2017

BALBOA
PRESS
A DIVISION OF HAY HOUSE

To Dearest Gursimran
Who Was Sometimes My Rock,
And Sometimes My Tree.

FOREWORD

I was delighted to be asked to write this foreword for Sharon who I first met in 2011 when it was my pleasure as Course Co-ordinator of the Master of Counselling and Psychotherapy at the Cairnmillar Institute, to welcome her as a student into the program. By the time of her initial interview, she had already written the screen play for a short film about Mental Illness entitled "Another World", and had completed placements in the area of Mental Health/Disability Law.

Sharon was an exemplary student, who demonstrated her fascination with the workings of the human psyche and shared herself generously with other students. At the 2013 graduation ceremony, she was awarded the Academic Excellence Award after consistently gaining top marks in her assessments and demonstrating strong academic and practical skills. She studied Existential Psychotherapy under my guidance and grasped the concepts in all their depth and breadth enthusiastically.

To complete her Masters degree in 2014, I had the happy task of supervising Sharon's Qualitative Research Thesis entitled *"The Client Experience of Discussing their Subjective Psychotic Experiences with Mental Health Professionals"* that as well as achieving a First Class Honours result, has made a valuable contribution to knowledge in a way that has practical implications.

Upon graduating, Sharon worked in Adult Mental Health in a support role, and has experience as a Child and Adolescent Counsellor, working with clients presenting with a wide range of issues. Sharon's passion for this work was ignited through the placement she undertook during her Masters training, where she was able to practice and enhance her skill in assisting the healthy emotional and psychological development of children.

As the great existentialist thinker Irvin Yalom (1980) in his book *Existential Psychotherapy* states "Any subject can be taught effectively in some intellectually honest form to any child at any stage of development" (P.105). This book achieves just that. While maintaining a simple and easy to follow narrative, the story of the Rock and Tree is an imaginative journey into profound questions of existence. Symbolically representative of timelessness and the struggle of all life for survival and expression, the story confronts some difficult concepts. Life is not always light and smooth sailing, and as with fairy tales such as "Grimm's Fairy tales" there is a dark side to the story of the Rock and Tree.

A first principle of existential philosophy is that existence is relational, and within this story there are many perspectives and interpretations of meaning possible, particularly when looking at this relational aspect. The sapling's behaviour towards the rock evokes strong feelings and it is easy to idealise the actions of rock and characterise the overall situation in simple terms of victim and perpetrator. However, this is challenged in the narrative through the anthropomorphic element that brings in human capacities for transcendence, love, selflessness, and questions about choice, freedom and responsibility, and ultimately death.

This book is a testament to Sharon's knowledge, life experience, and desire to engage in sharing her learning in a way that will support and nourish the growth of others.

Associate Professor Dr. Jane Power, MAPS, PACFA reg. clinical, ACRC, MSCAPE

INTRODUCTION

A Note for Child Therapists, Teachers and Parents:

This book is for general reading to/with children or adolescents or can be used as a tool in Child Therapy as it aligns well with Existential Theory. That is, this book provides a medium and context in which to raise and explore the ultimate Existential concerns of isolation, death, meaninglessness and freedom (and associated responsibility).

The main character, Rock, experiences loneliness or isolation and consequent sadness and a sense of unworthiness due to his personal characteristics and own self-image or self-perception. Rock perceives certain freedoms, demonstrated in the life-altering choices he makes. Through these choices, Rock takes on a grave and noble responsibility for another – Tree. Through the choices Rock makes, and the reasons he has for making these choices, Rock undergoes a journey of confronting meaninglessness and developing meaning for his existence. Rock also confronts his own death anxiety and fear of death. Ultimately, Rock finds meaning even in his own demise.

This book, in this way, is also life-affirming and validates Rock's actions based in love. This book contains many metaphors (rock, tree, river and pebbles) and has the potential value for child or adolescent readers of helping them understand: difficult or unreciprocated friendships and relationships; the impact of poor self-image and self-esteem; that we have freedoms to choose but these choices have consequences; how to combat meaninglessness in dire circumstances; how love can override reason; and the process of both fear and courage in facing one's mortality.

Author of *Therapeutic Storytelling: 101 Healing Stories for Children*, Susan Perrow (2012), explained, "A healing tale should, as much as possible, leave the listener free to come to her or his own conclusion – in this way the 'power of story' is left to work its own magic" (p.5). To help child readers engage in this process, however, I suggest that therapists, teachers or parents pose certain questions to the children they care for. For example: 'Why did Rock make the choices he did?'; 'Why did Rock get angry with the pebbles?'; 'Do either Rock or Tree remind you of anyone you know?'; or 'How could the story have ended differently?' The exploration is endless! Enjoy!

Please note: This story was originally written in 2004! The above analysis was a product of retrospective reflection. Hopefully this gives you additional permission to generate your own meanings for this story!

Sharon Williams
BA, LLB(Hons), MCPy

Once upon a time there was a very sad and lonely rock. The rock lived close to a rapid and raging river.

The rock's loneliness developed because none of the plants and animals by the river paid any attention to him.

The rock's sadness was caused by the knowledge that he was inanimate - that he would never change or grow of his own volition.

The rock felt totally worthless and spent his days wondering how he fitted into the world around him and what he could give.

For many years the rock just stayed by the river feeling sad and lonely. Then one day a small green shoot, a young tree sapling, began to grow next to the rock. The rock fell instantly in love - he had never seen anything so perfect in colour and so delicate in form in his entire life. The plant had a captivating fragility that contrasted starkly with the cold harshness the rock perceived in himself.

The sapling was close enough to touch the rock but it never did. The rock observed that the sapling often became tired as it struggled to grow, but that it never leaned on the rock for support.

Eventually the rock summoned the courage to ask the sapling why this was so. The rock had never before spoken to the sapling. "Why do you not rest your leaves on me when you are tired of growing?" questioned the sad rock.

The rock's low voice startled the young sapling; it did not know that rocks could talk. The sapling took one look at the rock and promptly turned away, completely ignoring the rock's question.

The rock said nothing more to the sapling but watched it as it grew. However one day the rock realised that the sapling was stretching its roots towards the river and thus growing towards the water each day. The rock instantly became very fearful for the young tree.

The rock knew that the river would drown the sapling when the rainy season arrived. He told the sapling this, but the sapling would not listen. It stubbornly continued to grow its roots towards the river, further and further away from any chance of safety.

The rock helplessly watched the ill-fated plant. Finally, he resolved that he would not let the poor, stubborn sapling die. The rock suddenly knew that the only way to save the sapling he loved was to roll into the river in front of it, thus redirecting the flow of water. So that is what he did.

The rainy season came and the water rose. The rock's young sapling was saved while many others along the river drowned. Still the young sapling did not speak to the rock or acknowledge his help.

"Didn't you see all the other saplings that drowned?" shouted the rock to the sapling, losing his temper. "I saved your life."

The sapling just nonchalantly turned away from the rock and continued to ignore him. The rock lowered his voice, "Please talk to me, young tree. I want you to be my friend."

The sapling stopped ignoring the rock for a moment and rudely replied "You are a waste of space, you are ugly and charcoal - the colour that all trees fear - I could never be friends with you."

"But does it not matter to you that I saved your life?" asked the rock. "You didn't save my life," countered the sapling, growing its roots more strongly into the water as it spoke, "I am strong and I would have survived the river."

At this infuriating remark, the rock was tempted to roll right out of the river and onto the bank, forcing the proud young tree to battle the gushing river by itself. But the rock did not move - he still loved the sapling for its intrinsic beauty and believed it would one day appreciate him.

So the rock decided to stay in the river to protect the young tree for another year.

A gurgle came from the water that surrounded the rock. It was a voice not of one but of hundreds in unison. "Beware," came the haunting message, "go back to shore while you still can. Save *YOURSELF.*"

The rock looked into the river and saw it was the pebbles on the river floor that were speaking to him. "Be quiet," yelled the rock, "I'm trying to save something beautiful and you are only asking me to destroy it." "No," insisted the pebbles, "we are telling you not to destroy yourself for an ungrateful creature." "You must listen to us," they pleaded, "we know what you are and what is your fate."

The rock did not understand the pebbles' cryptic comments, so he refused to listen to them. "Shut up," he yelled at their every attempt to speak, and eventually they gave up and were quiet for some time.

So the rock stayed in the water for another year while the tree was still too young to be beside the river alone. The sapling still refused to grow towards the shore and continued to have friendships only with other trees and plants but never with the poor rock.

When the wet season came again, the river was relentless and belted against the rock with great ferocity. Each wave of water was as painful as a whip, but the rock bore it for the sake of the young tree.

Each time the water ran over the rock, more particles of rock would erode from his surface. The rock had no knowledge of this occurring; he only experienced that he was in a lot of pain.

"Save yourself, save yourself," the pebbles continued to yell from the depths of the river, "get out while you can." But the rock would not budge and he did not plan to do so until he was satisfied that the beautiful tree he loved was safe.

So the rock stayed; he did not even try to move. Year after year the water ripped at his surface. The young sapling grew in height and girth until it became a tree, and all the while the loving rock watched in awe and suffered silently in order to protect it.

"Quick", yelled the pebbles loudly, "soon it will be too late." The rock heard what the pebbles were saying and this time he questioned them, "Too late for what?" The pebbles did not reply.

After
years...

After
years...

Years...

After
years...

One day, the rock, who had begun his protection of the tree with most of his mass well above the river level, suddenly noticed that he was barely high enough to break the water's surface.

He realised his plight and what all the pain throughout the years had been - that through erosion he was slowly shrinking - and suddenly he was scared. What had he done to himself?

"All will be okay," he told himself, "all I need to do is roll out of the river just as I rolled into it those many years ago." This was, regrettably, not the case.

The rock tried to move out of the deadly wetness but was now too small to generate enough momentum.

He could not move, even by an inch.

Without a doubt, he was stuck - trapped in that horrible river.

For the first time in his existence, the sad, lonely, selfless rock cried out for help. "Please," he begged the tree, "please help me." The tree made no reply. The rock tried again; "Please, if you use your roots you will be able to roll me back onto the bank of the river." Again the tree made no reply.

It was in fact true that the tree could hear all of the rock's cries and it was in fact possible for the tree to use its roots to save the rock. Nevertheless, despite all the rock had suffered in aid of the tree, the tree coldly and horribly ignored the pleas of the poor rock.

Time passed and soon the rock gave up his cries for help. In his naivety, the rock truly believed that the tree, which now towered high above him, could not hear him. The tree, of course, *could* hear him but because the tree believed it was superior and the rock ugly and inferior, it remained unmoved by the sight of the rock needlessly dying a slow and painful death.

Thus, after many, many more years of painful erosion, the rock finally ceased to exist. However, even in his last moments, just as he disintegrated and dispersed completely into mere tiny grains of sand, the rock watched the magnificent tree and was happy.

For, you see, the rock realised that it had come to matter little to him that his love for the tree was not returned. The rock recognised his own ugliness and appreciated the beauty that the world had given him to watch and protect. He died with some measure of happiness, because he had created a purpose for which to live, and it was of no consequence to him that he had received no gratitude or reward.

The last words the rock uttered were, "Goodbye, Tree."

goodbye tree

And just as he was washed away, he thought he heard a whisper through the branches and leaves ... "Goodbye, Rock."

THE END...

As you look at the rock at your feet, you see the rock, right then and there, as whole, complete and perfect. Yet even in the fraction of a moment that you hold that rock in your awareness, there is a lot going on within that rock - there is incredible movement, at incredible speed, of the particles of that rock. And what are those particles doing? They are making the rock what it is.

Neale Donald Walsch

www.ingramcontent.com/pod-product-compliance
Lightning Source LLC
Chambersburg PA
CBHW041132280526

45792CB00013B/2392